piano theory

By Mary Elizabeth Clark and David Carr Glover

PIANO LIBRARY

Materials Correlated with "The Piano Student" - Level V

Should the student not complete all of the correlated materials of LEVEL V by the time he has finished the "Piano Student" of that level, the teacher should continue to assign these materials with the "Piano Student," LEVEL VI. EARLY AMERICAN MUSIC, DUETS OF EARLY AMERICAN MUSIC, and BACH FOR PIANO ENSEMBLE recommended for LEVEL IV, can also be used with this level.

To The Student:

This book is a *"programed instruction"* Course of Study. Instead of paragraphs or pages of study and written work, there are small parts called "frames" that give information and ask you to make a written response.

You will find that everything you study in this book relates to the music that you are playing. The more that you understand about your music, the more you will enjoy playing it.

To The Teacher:

The Theory Books of the **DAVID CARR GLOVER PIANO LIBRARY** are written in "programed instruction" style, one of the most effective means of learning in modern education. Programed instruction is based on three generally accepted principles:

1. The material is presented in small steps called "frames."
2. The student makes an immediate written response to each frame so that his learning is constantly checked.
3. The student knows if his answer is correct.

The answers to the questions asked in the frames are on answer sheets in the back of the book. It depends upon the age of the student whether to have him use the answer sheets or have the teacher or parent check his answers. The answer sheets may be removed.

If the student uses the answer sheets, he is to cover the answers with a blank piece of paper moving the paper down to reveal each answer after he has written the response to each frame.

You will find the Post-Tests of all the books, and the Pre-Tests of all levels, except the Primer, most helpful in informing you of the student's progress and understanding.

It is highly recommended that you have the student do additional writing of new fundamentals on blank manuscript paper and that all Music Theory study be directly related to the literature being studied.

The Theory books are correlated to the **DAVID CARR GLOVER PIANO LIBRARY** but can be used with any Course or music of this level of advancement.

Contents

© 1971 Belwin Mills Publishing Corp. (ASCAP)
All Rights Assigned to and Controlled by Alfred Publishing Co., Inc.
All Rights Reserved including Public Performance. Printed in USA.

Pre-Test (Level V)

1. Change these Major Triads to Minor Triads.

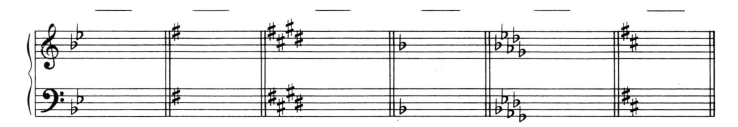

2. Change these Major Triads to Dominant Seventh Chords.

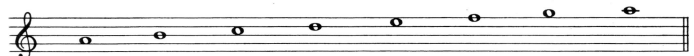

3. Write the Key-Note name over the staff of the following Major Key Signatures.

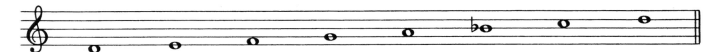

4. Add the necessary accidentals to form an A Major Scale.

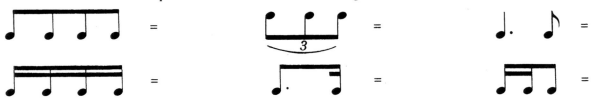

5. Add the necessary accidentals to form the D Harmonic Minor Scale from this Natural Minor Scale.

6. Write one note that equals the value of the notes given.

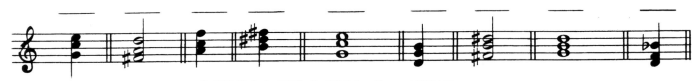

7. Add the upper note to complete each of these Harmonic Intervals.

8. Write the letter names above the staff of the ROOTS of these chords.

Pre-Test, Level V, Page 2

9. Write a chromatic scale from D to the next higher D.

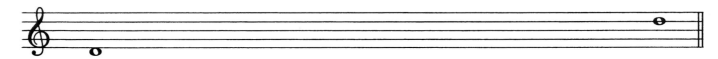

10. Write the name of the Major Key and the Relative Minor Key represented by the following Key Signatures.

Major Key _____   Major Key _____   Major Key _____

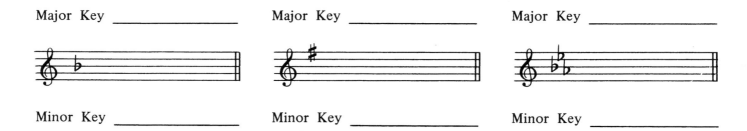

Minor Key _____   Minor Key _____   Minor Key _____

11. Write the following Major Key Signatures on both staffs.

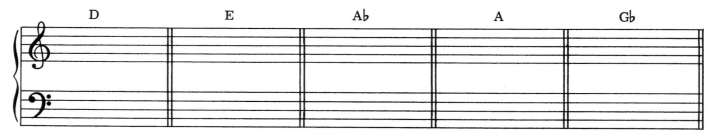

12. Change the following Minor Triads to Diminished Triads.

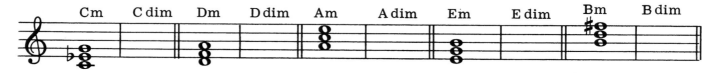

13. Change the following Major Triads to Augmented Triads.

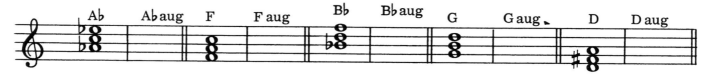

14. Write the chord symbol over each of the following Triads.

Example:

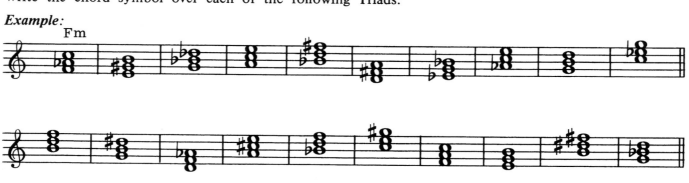

1. Music has form, design, and structure much like architecture, painting, and sculpture. The study of music is more meaningful and interesting when form is understood.

   A composition with two contrasting sections is written in **BINARY** or **Two-Part Form**. The first section is referred to as A and the second is B. An example of this Form is the *"Minuet"* by Haydn on Page 4 of the PIANO STUDENT, Level V.

   Complete these sentences.

   1. A composition with two contrasting sections is called _____ Form.

   2. The first section is called _____.

   3. The second section is called _____.

"Minuet", HAYDN
Piano Student, V

2. Write the beats under these measures of music.

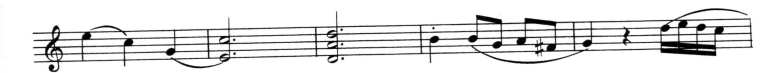

3. *Write the following Key Signatures on both staffs.

A Major	E Minor	B♭ Major	E♭ Major	B Major	D Minor

C Minor	D Major	F Minor	E Major	C Major	A Minor

*If necessary, refer to the Circle of Keys on the inside back cover.

_____

4. How many flats are in the Key of E Flat Major?_____

Write them in their correct order. _____

_____

5. How many flats in the Key of E Flat Major? _____

Write them in their correct order. _____

_____

6. What Major Key Signature has three sharps? _____

_____

7. What Major Key Signature has five flats? _____

8. The word Sonatina means a small Sonata. The Italian word Sonata means a piece of music that *"sounds"* on a musical instrument. Many early sonatas and sonatinas were written in Binary and Ternary Form (see Frame 9). About 1750 the Classical Sonata Form, which you will learn more about later, began to develop.

    1.   The Italian word Sonata means a piece of music that _____ on a musical instrument.

    2.   The word Sonatina means a small _____ .

    3.   The Classical Sonata Form began to develop about the year _____ .

    4.   Many early sonatas and sonatinas were written in _____ and _____

        Form.

---

9. TERNARY Form means a composition written in three sections. It is usually referred to as "Three-Part Song" Form. The first section is called A, the second section is B, and the third section is a repeat of A. The term is often shortened to "A–B–A" Form.

    1.   Three Part Song Form is called _____ Form.

    2.   The first section is called _____ .

    3.   The second section is called _____ .

    4.   The third section is called _____ .

---

10. A variation of the A–B–A Form is the A–A–B–A Form, often used for songs. A second repeated A section is sometimes varied slightly, such as being played an octave higher or lower.

    1.   A variation of the A–B–A Form is the _____ _____ _____ _____ Form.

    2.   This Form is often used for _____ .

    3.   The section that is sometimes varied is the repeated _____ section.

8

11. Quite often in music there are passages that seem to ask a question and passages that seem to answer the question. The question is called the Antecedent, and the answer is called the Consequent.

Play the following example.

Question (Antecedent)

Answer (Consequent)

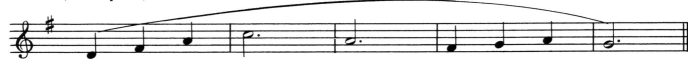

Write your answer to this musical question.

Question

Answer

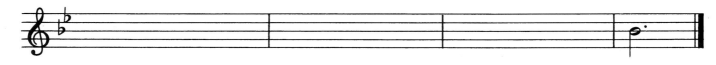

12. 1. The question passage of a piece is called the _____.

2. The answer passage of a piece is called the _____.

13 Write your answer to this musical question.

Question

Answer

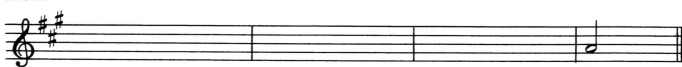

14. The following Triads are either Major or Minor. Write the chord symbols over the triads.

Example:

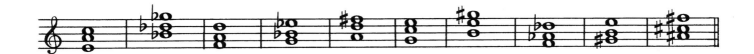

15. Write the chord symbols over these inverted Major and Minor Triads. The top note of the big skip is the ROOT.

Example:

16. An Augmented Triad is formed by raising the top note of a Major Triad one-half step.

Add the necessary accidentals to form Augmented Triads from these Major Triads.

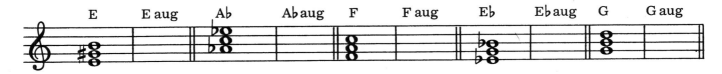

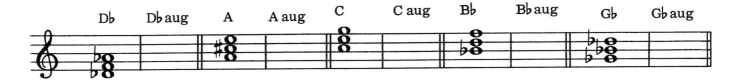

F.D.L.469

17. The following Triads are either Augmented or Major. Write the chord symbols over the Triads.

Example:

18. A Diminished Triad is formed by lowering the top note of a Minor Triad one-half step.

   Add the necessary accidentals to these Major and Minor Triads to form Diminished Triads.

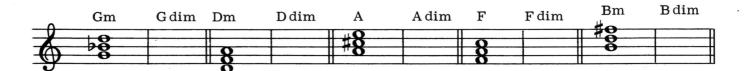

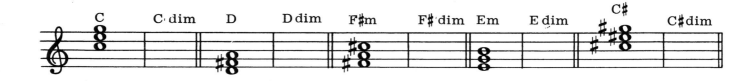

19. The following Triads are either Minor or Diminished. Write the chord symbols over the Triads.

20. Write the chord symbols over these Triads.

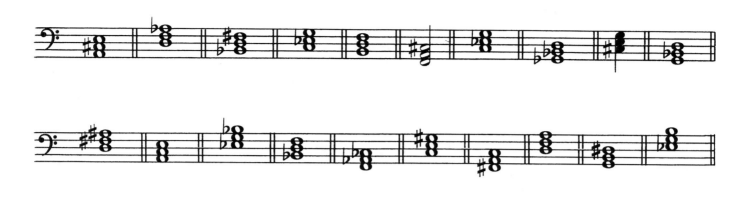

---

21. The Dominant Seventh Chord is formed by adding a note that is a Minor Third (1½ steps) above the top note of a Major Triad.

Write Dominant Seventh Chords from these Major Triads. Add the chord symbols over the chords.

Example:

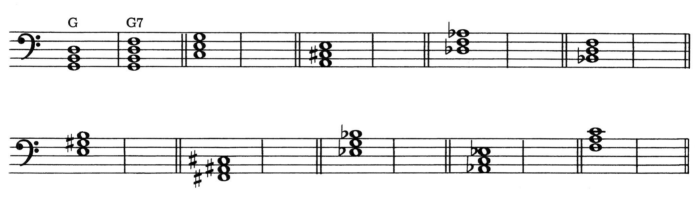

---

22. Dominant Seventh Chords may be inverted the same as Triads.

Root Position	*First Inversion*	*Second Inversion*	*Third Inversion*

Write the D7 chord and its three inversions as shown above.

Root Position	*First Inversion*	*Second Inversion*	*Third Inversion*

23. **3/8**   *METER SIGNATURE:*   **3** –   Three beats in each measure.

                                            8 –   An eighth note receives one beat.

Write the beats under these measures of music.

24. Add enough notes to complete these measures of music.

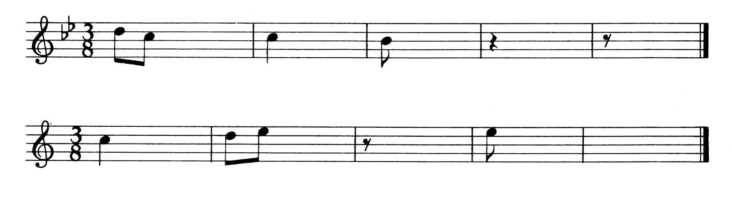

25. Add the Time Signature and then write the beats under these measures of music.

F.D.L.469

26. When a melody sung by one voice is repeated by a second voice starting on a later beat, it is called a CANON. A Canon may have more than two voices.

    Write the second voice of this Canon on the bass staff. The first and last measures have been completed for you. Follow the notes and the rhythm of the first voice. When you have completed the writing, play the piece on the piano.

    GURLITT

27. Write the second voice of this Canon on the treble staff. Follow the notes and the rhythm of the first voice. When you have completed the writing, play the Canon on the piano.

    KUNZ

28. The **PENTATONIC SCALE** uses only five tones. The easiest Pentatonic Scale to find on the keyboard is the one that begins on F sharp and uses the remaining four black keys.

Example:

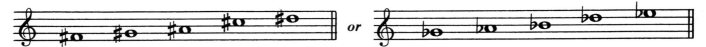

Play the Pentatonic Scale on the piano ascending and descending and listen. You will discover that it does not have the magnetic pull to a Tonic as the Major and Minor Scales do.

White keys are also used in some Pentatonic Scales. This is because of the arrangement of whole and half steps used in forming this scale. The Pentatonic Scale may begin on any note.

The pattern for a Pentatonic Scale is:

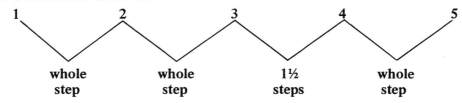

Write a Pentatonic Scale on each of these given notes.

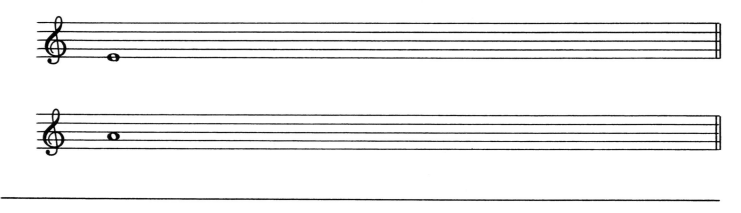

29. The following scale is a _____ scale.

'30. The following scale is a _____ _____ scale.

31. The following scale is a _____ _____ scale.

32. The following scale is a _____ scale.

33. The following scale is a _____ _____ scale.

34. The following scale is a _____ Scale.

35. Name the Triad and then write the first and second Inversions as shown in the example.

Example: F

36. **A SUITE** is a set of pieces in the same or related Keys often based on dance tunes. The Suite Form came to its fullest development during the Baroque Era, which was from about 1600 to 1750.

    Complete these sentences.
    1.   A set of pieces in the same or related Keys is called a _____ .

    2.   The Suite developed during the _____ Era.

    3.   The Baroque Era was from about 1600 to _____ .

37. The Baroque Suite usually consisted of at least four dances:

    (1) the allemande,   (2) courante,   (3) sarabande,   (4) and gigue.

    Complete this sentence:

    1.   Four dances usually included in the Baroque Suite were:

    (1) _____ ,   (2) _____ ,   (3) _____ , and (4) _____ .

38. In addition to the usual four dances of the Baroque Suite, optional dances such as the gavotte, minuet, and bourreé were used between the sarabande and gigue. Often a prelude preceded the Suite.

    Complete these sentences:

    1.   Optional dances sometimes used in a Baroque Suite were _____ , _____ , or _____ .

    2.   Sometimes a _____ preceded the entire suite.

    3.   The optional dances were usually used between the _____ and the _____ .

39. Johann Jacob Froberger (1616 – 1667) of Germany is usually credited with the origin of the Baroque Suite Form. He used the allemande, courante, and the sarabande as basic parts of his suites with the gigue, if used, in the middle between two of the other dances. Later some of his suites were published with the gigue as the final, climactic dance.

    Complete this sentence.

    The composer usually credited with the origin of the Baroque Suite Form is Johann Jacob _____ .

40. Johann Sebastian Bach adopted Froberger's form. In addition, Bach's suites and partitas contain one or more dances of the French type such as a bourrée, gavotte, minuet, or passepied.

Bach's suites and partitas are considered the highest development of the suite as an art form. (Partita means the same as a suite.)

Complete these sentences.

1. Johann Sebastian Bach included dances of the _____ type in his suites and partitas.

2. The highest development of the suite as an art form was done by Johann _____
   _____ .

---

41. The dances in a Baroque Suite may be described as follows:

Allemande	*German*	— moderate, serious, legato - four beats to the measure; (sometimes two long beats).
Bourrée	*French*	— lively , energetic - two beats to the measure.
Courante	*French*	— quick, even flow of notes, often has a variety of rhythms - three beats to the measure.
Corrente	*Italian*	— easy, fast, running pace, but not so complex as the French Courante - three beats to the measure.
Gavotte	*French*	— stately - four and sometimes two beats to the measure, generally beginning on the third beat of the measure.
Gigue	*French*	— light, rapid, developed from the 16th century Irish or English jig — $\frac{6}{8}$ or $\frac{12}{8}$ meter.
Giga	*Italian*	— the same distinction can be made between the French Gigue and the Italian Giga as between the French Courante and the Italian Corrente.
Menuet	*French*	— graceful, unhurried tempo - three beats to the measure (Minuet — English; Minuetto — Italian; Menuett — German).
Passepied	*French*	— gay, rapid motion - three beats to the measure.
Sarabande	*French*	— slow, stately - three beats to the measure.

1. The Allemande was of _____ origin.
2. The Gavotte usually begins on the _____ beat of the measure.
3. Menuett is the _____ spelling.

---

42. The use of the Suite Form during the Classical Period was rare. The Sonata was developing at this time. Later in the 19th century composers used the Suite Form again. Some examples are Grieg's *Peer Gynt Suites*, which were taken from a set of pieces that he had written for drama. Tchaikovsky's *Nutcracker Suite* was from ballet music. A modern Suite from opera is Kodaly's *Hary Janos* and another is from a ballet score, Stravinsky's *Firebird Suite*.

1. Famous Suites of Grieg's are the _____ _____ _____ .

A Sonata is a musical composition of several contrasting movements for one or two instruments. A symphony is a sonata for orchestra; a quartet is a sonata for four instruments; and a concerto is a sonata for a solo instrument and orchestra.

The term *sonata form or sonata-allegro form* refers to the design or plan frequently used in the first movement. It has three main parts: Exposition, Development, and Recapitulation. Each of these main parts has sections arranged according to Key relationships (see chart below). The **EXPOSITION**, in which the composer's ideas are first exposed, may start with a brief Introduction, but usually goes right into the **FIRST THEME** in the Tonic Key. Sometimes more than one theme is heard, but all stay in the Tonic or Home Key. A bridge or transition (optional) leads to the **SECOND THEME** (or themes) in a closely related Key (normally the Dominant, but if the home Key is minor, the Relative Major). Next there may be a series of short episodes, or a closing theme, or both, ending in a final cadence in the new key. This is where the double bar with repeat marks is found leading to the

DEVELOPMENT, using themes from the Exposition, varying and combining them, and modulating quickly through different Keys, usually by a series of sequences. The last part of the Development stresses the original Dominant, bridging over into the

RECAPITULATION, which repeats the same material heard in the Exposition in the same order. This time, however, all of the material stays in the original Tonic Key. Sometimes a Coda, usually based on previous themes, is added at the very end.

The overall tonal plan may be compared to a journey: in the **EXPOSITION** one spends a little time in the home state, such as Iowa, (Tonic, or home Key; **FIRST THEME** (s)). Then one goes (transition) to a bordering state for a while (Related Key: **SECOND THEME** (s), episodes, closing theme). In the **DEVELOPMENT** one passes through several states, spending only a short time in each; the last one (Dominant) is again a border state. In the **RECAPITULATION** one spends all the rest of the trip in the home state (Tonic).

In the above description and the chart, the essential parts of the form are in **CAPITALS**, and sections in small type. In a Sonatina or a short sonata some of the sections in small print may be omitted (this does not necessarily mean that it is technically easier than a longer sonata, however).

Most keyboard sonatas have three movements. The second movement is usually slow and lyrical. The third movement is often the fastest of the movements and may end in a fanfare and climax. Many third movements are written in Rondo form.

The Sonatina by Oskar Block on Page 22 of the **"Piano Student"**, **V**, follows the outline of sonata-allegro form. The second movement is slower than the first or third. The third movement is ABAB form with the first B theme in the Dominant Key and the final B theme in the Tonic Key.

You will find it interesting to analyze the form of other sonatinas and sonatas that you study or hear.

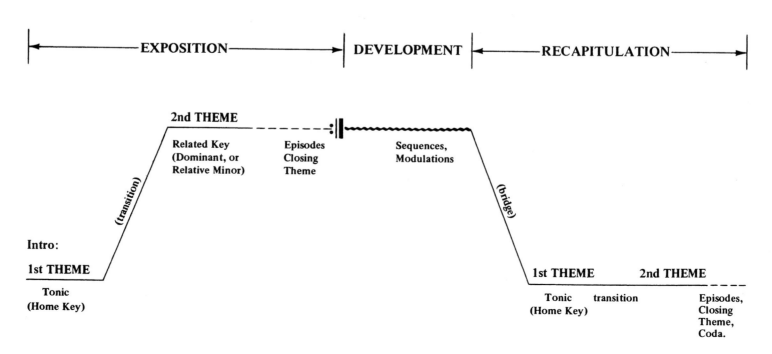

43. 1. The term **sonata-allegro form** refers to the plan frequently used in the _____ move-

     ment of a sonata.

     2. The first movement of the sonata has _____ main Parts.

     3. The first Part is called the _____, the second Part is called the _____,

     and the third Part is called the _____ .

---

44. 1. The first Theme of the Exposition of **sonata-allegro form** is in the _____ Key.

     2. The second Theme of the Exposition is in a _____ Key.

     3. Themes in the Development Part are developed through means of sequences and _____ _____ .

     4. The first Theme of the Recapitulation is in the _____ Key.

     5. The second Theme of the Recapitulation is in the _____ Key.

---

45. The ascending chromatic scale is usually written with sharps.

   Example:

   Write a chromatic scale from the first given F to the next given F one octave higher.

---

46. The descending chromatic scale is usually written with flats.

   Example:

   Write a chromatic scale from the first given G to the next given G one octave lower.

47. The notation of rhythm developed over many centuries. It is helpful to know some music history on this subject to better understand the terms that you are using in your music study.

Many of the rhythmical terms used are Italian, French, or British words rather than American. The chart below gives the British terms for kinds of notes. You will find this useful in studying such terms as **Alla Breve.**

Before 1700 Mensural notation was used for rhythm, which was one of the earliest ways of indicating definite values of notes. Long and short notes and their relation to each other were shown. However, bar lines were rare and Meter Signatures as we know them did not exist. During this time the use of a complete **O** for *"perfect"* meter, or a rhythm of three, was used; and the *"imperfect,"* or rhythm of four, was shown by a broken circle **C**. This sign is still in use today, meaning $\frac{4}{4}$ meter, a Meter Signature that is often referred to as *"common time."* Historians do not all agree as to the meaning of *"perfect time."* Some have said that three was the rhythm most used in poetry and that poetry had much to do with music then. Others have referred to three as meaning *"The Trinity."* The main point to remember is that the complete circle meant three and the broken circle meant four.

Since about 1700 our familiar system of Meter Signatures has been used, and it is called Metrical or Measured rhythm.

¢ – Alla Breve comes from the Italian meaning *"to shorten."* A vertical stroke or line down through the center of the **C** indicates this rhythm, which was used early in measured music. It is often referred to as *"cut time."* The line means that each note is to be halved in time value or the movement doubled. Music marked with alla breve is usually performed twice as fast as if simply marked with the sign **C** or $\frac{4}{4}$. This is the same as $\frac{2}{2}$ meter. It is important to think of the half note receiving one beat or pulse. Many hymns are written in $\frac{2}{2}$ meter.

In music the term Time Signature is often used in place of Meter Signature. The word time in many other instances is used when in fact the word meter should have been used.

KINDS OF NOTES

AMERICAN USAGE	SYMBOL	BRITISH USAGE
Two tied whole notes	**o͜o** or ⊨ or ‖o‖	Breve
Whole Note	**o**	Semibreve
Half Note	𝅗𝅥	Minim
Quarter Note	♩	Crotchet
Eighth Note	♪	Quaver
Sixteenth Note	𝅘𝅥𝅯	Semiquaver
Thirty-second note	𝅘𝅥𝅰	Demi-semiquaver

1. Mensural rhythm notation was used before the year _____.

2. Since about 1700 our familiar system of Meter Signatures and bar lines has been used, and it is called_____ or _____ rhythm.

48. Complete these sentences.

    1. The complete **O** indicated "perfect meter," which was a rhythm of _____.

    2. The broken circle **C** meant _____ meter, which was a rhythm of four.

    3. The broken circle is still in use today meaning _____ beats in each measure. It is often referred to as "_____ time."

---

49. 1. Alla Breve comes from the Italian meaning _____ _____.

    2. This rhythm is indicated by a vertical _____ through the center of the **C**.

    3. Alla Breve is the same as _____ _____ meter.

    4. The **¢** Meter Signature indicates _____ beats in each measure. It is often referred to as "_____ time."

    5. The kind of note receiving one pulse in alla breve time is the _____ note.

---

50. Complete this list.

    The British words for the following kinds of notes are:

    Whole Note — _____.

    Half Note — _____.

    Quarter Note — _____.

    Eighth Note — _____.

    Sixteenth Note — _____.

---

51. **2/2**   *METER SIGNATURE:*   **2** – Two beats in each measure.
    2 – A half note receives one beat.

    Write the beats under these measures of music.

52. A Diatonic Scale uses every letter name in order, ascending or descending, and does not repeat a letter name or skip a letter name.

As you learned in **Piano Theory**, Level Four, each degree of a Diatonic Scale has a specific Roman Numeral and a specific name.

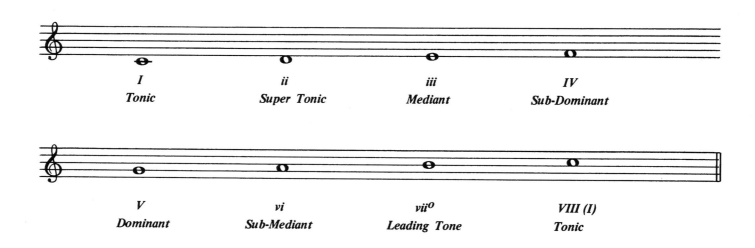

I	*ii*	*iii*	*IV*
Tonic	Super Tonic	Mediant	Sub-Dominant

V	*vi*	*vii°*	*VIII (I)*
Dominant	Sub-Mediant	Leading Tone	Tonic

1.   The first degree (I) of a Diatonic Scale is called the _____.

2.   The fourth degree (IV) of a Diatonic Scale is called the _____ _____.

3.   The fifth degree (V) of a Diatonic Scale is called the _____.

---

53. The large Roman Numerals indicate that the Triad built on that degree of a Major Scale is a Major Triad.

Write the large Roman Numerals under the Tonic, Sub-Dominant, and Dominant degrees of these Major Scales.

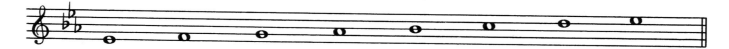

54.   1.   The second degree (ii) of a Major Scale is called the _____ _____ .

       2.   The third degree (iii) of a Major Scale is called the _____ .

       3.   The sixth degree (vi) of a Major Scale is called the _____ _____ .

       4.   The seventh degree (vii°) of a Major Scale is called the _____ _____ .

---

55.   The small Roman Numerals indicate that the Triad built on that degree of a Major Scale is a Minor Triad.

Write the small Roman Numerals under the Super-Tonic, Mediant, and Sub-Mediant degrees of this scale.

---

56.   The small Roman Numeral with the small circle following indicates that the Triad built on this degree of a Major Scale is a Diminished Triad.

Write the Roman Numeral and circle indicating Diminished under the Leading-Tone of this Major scale.

---

57.   The chords built on the first, fourth, and fifth degrees of the Major Scale (I, IV, and V) are the **Primary** Chords of the Key. They form the basic structure of our harmonic tonal system.

       1.   The chords built on I, IV, and V are the _____ Chords of the Key.

       2.   They form the basic structure of our _____ tonal system.

---

58.   The chords built on the second, third, sixth, and seventh degrees of the Major Scale (ii, iii, vi, and vii°) are called the **Secondary** Chords of the Key.

The chords built on the ii, iii, vi, and vii° degrees of the Major Scale are called the _____ Chords of the Key.

24

59. Write the Roman numerals under each of these chords.

Key of F Major

Key of E Major

60. Write the Key Signature as indicated.

Write the Triad in Root Position as indicated by the Roman Numerals.

Key of D Major

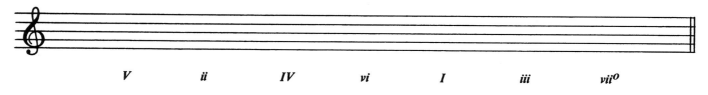

       V   *ii*   *IV*   *vi*   *I*   *iii*   *vii°*

Key of B Flat Major

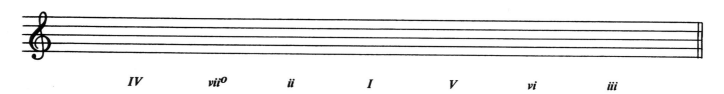

       IV   *vii°*   *ii*   *I*   *V*   *vi*   *iii*

Key of A Major

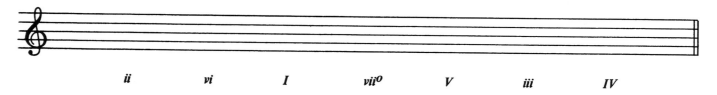

       ii   *vi*   *I*   *vii°*   *V*   *iii*   *IV*

Key of F Major

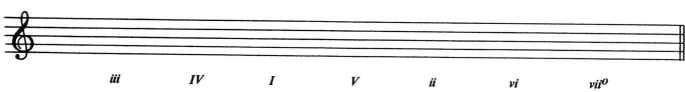

       iii   *IV*   *I*   *V*   *ii*   *vi*   *vii°*

61. Write the number name under each of these Harmonic intervals.

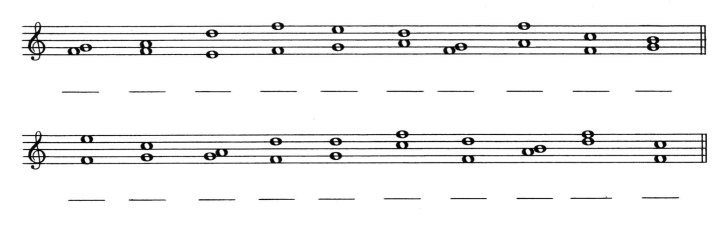

___ ___ ___ ___ ___ ___ ___ ___ ___

___ ___ ___ ___ ___ ___ ___ ___ ___

62. The intervals built on the tones of a Major Scale are either Perfect or Major.

Example:

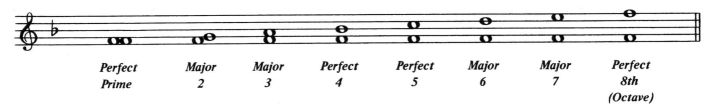

| Perfect Prime | Major 2 | Major 3 | Perfect 4 | Perfect 5 | Major 6 | Major 7 | Perfect 8th (Octave) |

Write Perfect or Major and the Number Names of these Intervals.

Example:

Major ___ ___ ___ ___ ___ ___ ___

3 ___ ___ ___ ___ ___ ___ ___

63. Write the beats under these measures of music.

64. The WHOLE-TONE Scale is all whole steps with six whole steps within one octave. A whole-tone scale may begin on any note. There are only two whole-tone scales, but they have several different spellings. They may be written as follows:

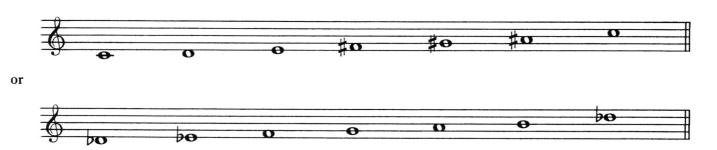

or

Add the necessary sharps or flats to form Whole-Tone Scales.

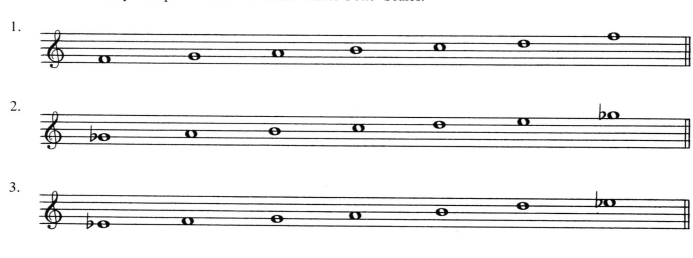

1.

2.

3.

---

65. Claude Debussy (1862–1918) was the first composer to use the Whole-Tone Scale extensively. Many composers have used it since his time.

The first composer to use the Whole-Tone Scale a great deal was _____ _____.

---

66. Write your answer to this musical question.

Question

Answer

67. Write your answer to this musical question.

Question

Answer

68. Write the beats under these measures of music, using "ands".

69. Write the Key-Note letter name over the staff of these Major Key Signatures.

Example:

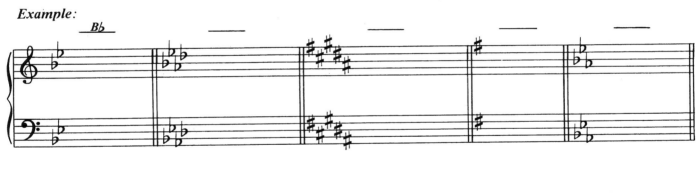

70. Although the Key-notes of relative Major and Minor Keys are different, the Key Signatures are the same. The Key Signature, therefore, *does not* indicate whether the composition is Major or Minor.

Example:

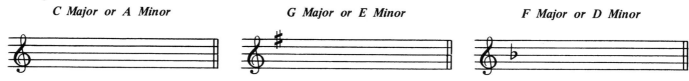

The Key of a piece is determined by the melody and harmonies used. Music in a Major Key usually begins and ends on one or more notes of the Tonic Major Chord of the Major Scale. Music in a Minor Key usually begins and ends on one or more notes of the Tonic Minor Chord of the Minor Scale.

Example:

This music is in the Key of C Major because the beginning and ending notes belong to the Tonic C Major Chord.

This music is in the Key of A Minor because the beginning and ending notes belong to the Tonic A Minor Chord.

Write the Key name of the following examples and indicate Major or Minor.

Music that is not chordal has melodic intervals, harmonic intervals, and scale passages that reveal Major or Minor tonalities. Also, the last notes are usually a part of the Tonic Chord of the Key.

71. Write the Key names of the following examples under the staff indicating Major or Minor.

    Suggested procedure:
1. Look at the last measure of the piece and determine the Key-note.
2. Look at the Key Signature at the beginning of the piece.
3. Analyze the harmony, melody, or both of the first two or three measures.

1. Key: _____

2. Key: _____

3. Key: _____

4. Key: _____

72. Write the Key names of the following examples under the staff indicating Major or Minor.

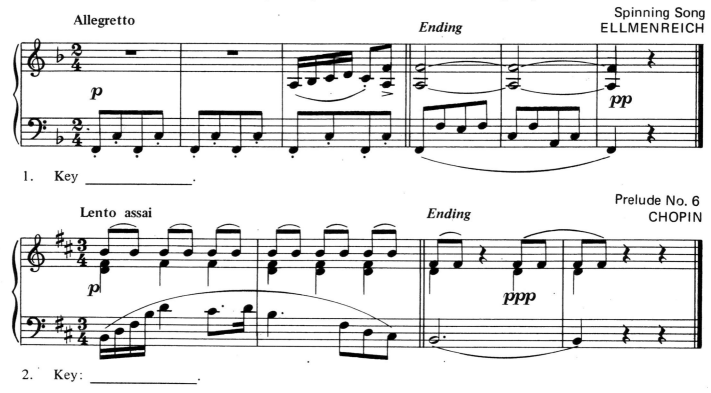

Allegretto *Ending* Spinning Song ELLMENREICH

1. Key _____.

Lento assai *Ending* Prelude No. 6 CHOPIN

2. Key: _____.

---

73. $\frac{5}{8}$ *METER SIGNATURE:* **5** — Five beats in each measure.

8 — An eighth note receives one beat.

Irregular rhythms such as $\frac{5}{8}$ and $\frac{7}{8}$ often have a feeling of sub-division within the measure. The following excerpt from "Toccatina" indicates a pattern of 3 and then 2. Sometimes these are indicated in parenthesis after the Meter Signature..

Example: $\frac{5}{8}$ $^{(3-2)}_{8}$ *or* $\frac{7}{8}$ $^{(3-4)}_{8}$ Toccatina — GLOVER
Piano Student, V

Write the beats under these measures of music, counting to 5.

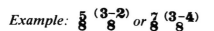

Sometimes a student finds it helpful to count 1-2-3, 1-2 for this kind of rhythm.

Write the beats under these measures of music counting 1-2-3, 1-2.

Post-Test, Level V

1. Add the upper note to complete each of these Harmonic Intervals.
   Example:

   7   6   3   2   8   4   5   3

2. Write the following Major Key Signatures on both staffs.

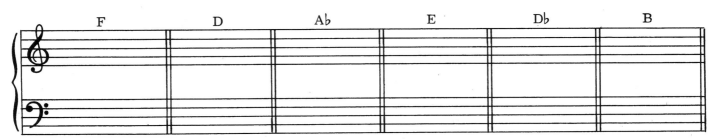

3. A composition with two contrasting sections is called _____ Form.

4. A composition with three sections is called _____ Form.

5. Write your answer to this musical question.

6. Write the chord symbols over these triads.
   Example: F

7. In ³⁄₈ Time the eighth note receives _____ beat and the quarter note receives _____ beats.

8. A melody sung by one voice and repeated by a second voice starting on a later beat is called a _____.

9. The following scale is a _____ Minor Scale.

10. The Pentatonic Scale uses only _____ tones.

11. Write a Pentatonic Scale on the given note.

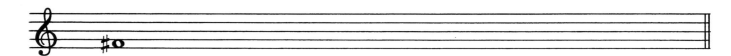

12. Name any four of the dances used in the Baroque Suite.

    1. _____   2. _____   3. _____   4. _____

13. The term **sonata-allegro form** refers to the plan frequently used in the _____ movement

    of a sonata.

14. There are _____ main Parts in the **sonata-allegro form**.

15. Our familiar system of Time Signatures has been in existence since about the year _____.

16. **C** or $\frac{4}{4}$ Time Signature is often called _____ Time.

17. In $\frac{2}{8}$ Time Signature the _____ note receives one beat.

18. The fourth degree of a diatonic scale is called the _____ _____.

19. Large Roman numerals indicate _____ chords and small Roman numerals indicate _____

    chords.

20. Intervals built on the tones of a Major Scale are either Perfect or _____.

21. Write the Key name of the following example under the staff and indicate Major or Minor.

    Key: _____

22. Add the necessary sharps or flats to form a whole-tone scale.

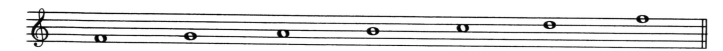

Answers (Level V)

PRE-TEST

1.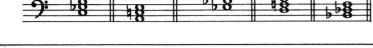

2.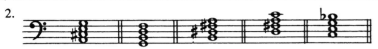

3. Bb, G, E, F, Db, D

4.

5.

6.

7.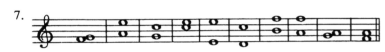

8. C, D, F, B, C, G, B, G, Bb

9.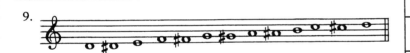

10. F,   G,   Eb
    D Minor, E Minor, C Minor

11.

12.

13.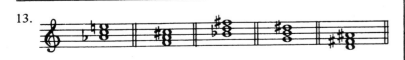

14. Fm, E, G dim, Am, Bb aug, D, Eb, Ab aug, G, Cm
    B dim, G aug, D dim, A, Bb, C aug, F, Em, B, Gm

FRAMES

1. 1. Binary   2. A   3. B

2.

3.

4. four   F C G D

5. three   Bb Eb Ab

6. A

7. D Flat

8. 1. sounds 2. Sonata 3. 1750 4. Binary, Ternary

9. 1. Ternary 2. A 3. B 4. A

10. 1. A-A-B-A 2. songs 3. A

11.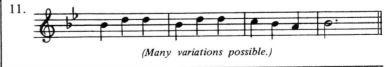

    (Many variations possible.)

12. 1. Antecedent 2. Consequent

13.

    (Many variations possible.)

F.D.L.469

Answers, Level V, Page 2

14. Ab, F#m, G, Gm, A, F#, Gm, Bbm, E, Bb
    B, C, Dm, Bm, Eb, Cm, Fm, Db, Gb, Am

15. Cm, D, Bb, A, F, Eb, Db, E, Gm, B
    Am, Gb, Dm, Eb, D, C, E, Db, E, F#

16.

17. E, C aug, F aug, Db aug, G, Eb, A, E, Bb aug
    F aug, B, F#, C aug, G, Gb aug, Eb aug, A, Ab aug

18.

19. B dim, D dim, Cm, Ebm, D dim, Em, Em, Fm, Fm, B dim
    F# dim, Cm, Gm, Dm, Am, Em, Bbm, G dim, Bm, A dim

20. A, D dim, Bb aug, Cm, B dim, F aug, Cm, Gb aug, C# dim, Gm
    D aug, Am, Eb, Bb, F dim, C aug, F# dim, Dm, G aug, Eb aug

21.

22.

23.

24.

(Other combinations possible.)

25.

26.

27.

28.

29. Major

30. Natural Minor

31. Harmonic Minor

32. Chromatic

33. Melodic Minor

34. Pentatonic

35.

52. 1. Tonic   2. Sub-Dominant   3. Dominant

53.

36. 1. Suite   2. Baroque   3. 1750

37 1. allemande   2. courante   3. sarabande   4. gigue

38. 1. gavotte, minuet, bourrée   2. prelude   3. sarabande, gigue

39. Froberger

40. 1. French   2. Sebastian Bach

41. 1. German   2. third   3. German

42. Peer Gynt Suites

43. 1. first   2. three 3. Exposition, Development, Recapitulation

44. 1. Tonic 2. Related   3. Key changes 4. Tonic   5. Tonic

45.

46.

47. 1. 1700   2. Metrical, Measured

48. 1. three   2. imperfect   3. four, common

49. 1. to shorten   2. line   3. two two   4. 2, cut   5. half

50. semibreve, minim, crotchet, quaver, semiquaver

51.

54. 1. Super Tonic 2. Mediant 3. Sub-Mediant 4. Leading Tone

55.

56.

57. 1. Primary   2. harmonic

58. Secondary

59.

60.

61. 2, 3, 7, 8, 6, 4, 2, 6, 5, 3
7, 4, 2, 6, 5, 4, 6, 2, 3, 5

62.

Major	Perfect	Major	Perfect	Major
3	5	7	4	2

Perfect	Major	Major	Perfect	Major
8	6	3	5	2

Answers, Level V, Page 4

63.

64.

65. Claude Debussy

66.

(Many variations possible.)

67.

(Many variations possible.)

68.

69. Bb, Ab, B, G, Eb
A, Db, D, C♯
F, Gb, E, Bb, C

70. G Major, E Minor
F Major, D Minor

71. 1. E Minor 2. G Minor 3. Eb Major 4. A Minor

72. F Major
B Minor

73.

POST-TEST

1.

2.

3. Binary

4. Ternary

5.

(Many variations possible.)

6. F, A dim, Bb, Bb aug, Am, Cm, G, Db aug

7. one, two

8. Canon

9. Harmonic

10. five

11.

12. Any four of these: allemande, bourrée, courante, gavotte, gigue, menuet, passepied, sarabande.

13. first

14. three

15. 1700

16. Common

17. half

18. Sub-Dominant

19. Major, Minor

20. Major

21. B Minor

22.

F.D.L.469